World Almanac® Library of American Immigration

Arab
Americans

Marilyn D. Anderson

Curriculum Consultant: Michael Koren,
Social Studies Teacher, Maple Dale School, Fox Point, Wisconsin

WORLD ALMANAC® LIBRARY

Please visit our web site at: www.garethstevens.com
For a free color catalog describing World Almanac® Library's list of
high-quality books and multimedia programs, call 1-800-848-2928 (USA)
or 1-800-387-3178 (Canada). World Almanac® Library's fax: (414) 332-3567.

Library of Congress Cataloging-in-Publication Data

Anderson, Marilyn D.
     Arab Americans / by Marilyn D. Anderson.
         p. cm. – (World Almanac Library of American immigration)
     Includes bibliographical references and index.
     ISBN-10: 0-8368-7307-6 – ISBN-13: 978-0-8368-7307-8 (lib. bdg.)
     ISBN-10: 0-8368-7320-3 – ISBN-13: 978-0-8368-7320-7 (softcover)
     1. Arab Americans–History–Juvenile literature.   2. Arab Americans–Social
conditions–Juvenile literature.   3. Immigrants–United States–History–Juvenile literature.
     4. Arab countries–Emigration and immigration–History–Juvenile literature.   5. United
States–Emigration and immigration–History–Juvenile literature. I. Title. II. Series.
     E184.A65A454   2007
     973'.04927–dc22   2006011370

First published in 2007 by
World Almanac® Library
A member of the WRC Media Family of Companies
330 West Olive Street, Suite 100
Milwaukee, WI 53212, USA

Produced by Discovery Books
Editor: Jim Mezzanotte
Designer and page production: Sabine Beaupré
Photo researcher: Sabrina Crewe
Maps and diagrams: Stefan Chabluk
Consultant: Elsa Marston
World Almanac® Library editorial direction: Mark J. Sachner
World Almanac® Library editor: Carol Ryback
World Almanac® Library design: Scott M. Krall
World Almanac® Library art direction: Tammy West
World Almanac® Library production: Jessica Morris

Picture credits: Cover: Topfoto/Image Works; title page: Topfoto/Image Works; 5: Lucy
Nicholson/AFP/Getty Images; 7: Yves Gellie/CORBIS; 8: Nabeel Turner/Stone/Getty Images; 9:
Hulton Archive/Getty Images; 10: Roger Lemoyne/Liaison/Getty Images; 11: Nabil Ismail-Rabih
Moghrabi/AFP/Getty Images; 12: Bettmann/CORBIS; 14: Library of Congress; 15: John Phillips/
Time & Life Pictures/Getty Images; 16: William Williams Papers/Manuscripts & Archives Division,
The New York Public Library, Astor, Lenox & Tilden Foundations; 18: Immigration History Research
Center, University of Minnesota; 19: The New York Public Library, Astor, Lenox & Tilden
Foundations; 20: Bettmann/CORBIS; 23: Naff Collection/Archives Center/National Museum of
American History, Smithsonian Institution; 24: Library of Congress; 25: Library of Congress; 26:
The New York Public Library, Astor, Lenox & Tilden Foundations; 27: Immigration History Research
Center, University of Minnesota; 29: Bettmann/CORBIS; 31: David Rubinger/Time & Life
Pictures/Getty Images; 32: Rebecca Cook/Reuters /CORBIS; 33: Jeff Kowalsky/AFP/Getty Images;
34: Robyn Beck/AFP/Getty Images; 36: Ed Kashi/CORBIS; 37: FEMA; 39: Jim West/Topfoto/Image
Works; 40: Scott Cunningham/Getty Images; 41: Hulton Archive/Getty Images; 43:
Jeff Kowalsky/epa/CORBIS

Printed in the United States of America

1 2 3 4 5 6 7 8 9 10 09 08 07 06

Contents

Front cover: Like other U.S. citizens, Arab Americans take pride in their country.

Title page: Arab Americans in Dearborn, Michigan, read a newspaper that is in both Arabic and English.

Introduction

The United States has often been called "a nation of immigrants." With the exception of Native Americans—who have inhabited North America for thousands of years—all Americans can trace their roots to other parts of the world.

Immigration is not a thing of the past. More than seventy million people came to the United States between 1820 and 2005. One-fifth of that total—about fourteen million people—immigrated since the start of 1990. Overall, more people have immigrated permanently to the United States than to any other single nation.

Push and Pull

Historians write of the "push" and "pull" factors that lead people to emigrate. "Push" factors are the conditions in the homeland that convince people to leave. Many immigrants to the United States were—and still are—fleeing persecution or poverty. "Pull" factors are those that attract people to settle in another country. The dream of freedom or jobs or both continues to pull immigrants to the United States. People from many countries around the world view the United States as a place of opportunity.

Building a Nation

Immigrants to the United States have not always found what they expected. People worked long hours for little pay, often doing jobs that others did not want to do. Many groups also endured prejudice.

In spite of these challenges, immigrants and their children built the United States of America, from its farms, railroads, and computer industries to its beliefs and traditions. They have enriched American life with their culture and ideas. Although they honor their heritage, most immigrants and their descendants are proud to call themselves Americans first and foremost.

▲ Muslims in California hold a memorial service after the 9/11 terrorist attacks.

The Arab American Story

In many ways, the story of Arab immigration is different from other immigrant stories. Arabs have immigrated in smaller numbers than other groups. In addition, Arab Americans come from a variety of homelands, and they do not all have the same backgrounds. Some Arab immigrants, for example, have been Christian. Others have been Muslim. Yet many Arabs have shared the same traditions and the same reasons for moving to the United States. Like other immigrants, they had to overcome prejudice and other obstacles, and they have made important contributions to American life. Arab Americans have been scientists, doctors, business leaders, Hollywood entertainers, and athletes. They have also been farmers, factory workers, and small business owners.

Arab Americans still face many challenges. Relations between the United States and some Arab countries have often been strained. Terrorist attacks by Arab Muslim extremists, including the "9/11" attacks on September 11, 2001, have led many Americans to view Arabs with hostility and suspicion. The U.S. government now keeps close watch on the activities of some Arabs in its fight against terror. Most Arab Americans, however, have been as horrified by terrorism as all other Americans. They love the United States, and they want only to pursue the many opportunities it offers.

"There was a lot of people crying. I was so sad. There was a lot of people who cared a lot about the things that happened. And they love this country so much. This is a country that brings us all together. I came from Yemen when I was nine."

Nassar Al Subai, age thirteen, at an Arab candlelight vigil in New York City just after the 9/11 attacks

5

CHAPTER 1

Life in the Homeland

Nearly all Arabs come from the Middle East, a region that includes parts of southwest Asia and North Africa. Some Arab countries have borders on the shore of the Mediterranean Sea. Others are on the Arabian Peninsula, which is bordered on the west by the Red Sea and on the east by the Persian Gulf and the Arabian Sea. The Middle East has rugged mountains, vast deserts, and areas of fertile farmland.

The question of which countries are Arab can be a difficult one to answer, even among Arabs. Iran and Afghanistan, for example, are not considered Arab countries, though they are Muslim countries in the Middle East. In general, Arabs are united by a common language, culture, and history. Arab countries include Algeria, Bahrain, Egypt, Iraq, Jordan, Kuwait, Lebanon,

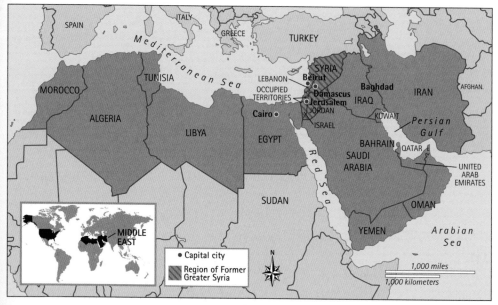

▲ This map shows some of the countries in what is often considered the Middle East.

▲ A restaurant in Damascus, Syria. The Middle East is a blend of old and new.

Morocco, Oman, Qatar, Saudi Arabia, Sudan, Syria, the United Arab Emirates, and Yemen.

A Long History

The Middle East is home to some of the world's earliest civilizations. More than six thousand years ago, people settled along the Nile River, in what is now Egypt. Ancient civilizations were also established between the Tigris and Euphrates Rivers, in what is now Iraq and Syria.

In the seventh century, Arabic-speaking people from the Arabian Peninsula, in what is now Saudi Arabia, began conquering much of the Middle East. They spread their culture, including their language and their newly founded religion, Islam. Among the places they conquered was Persia, which is now called Iran. Persia became Muslim, but it kept much of its culture, including its own language.

Although many Arabs settled in cities and villages, some Arabs were nomads. They roamed the deserts of North Africa and the Arabian Peninsula, moving from place to place as they herded camels, goats, and horses. Today, some Arabs are still nomads.

Greater Syria

Most Arab Americans trace their roots to Greater Syria, a region in the Middle East that is now made up of modern-day Lebanon, Syria, and Jordan, as well as Israel and the Palestinian territories.

The Religion of Islam

People who practice Islam are called Muslims. They believe in the same God as Christians and Jews, but their religion is based on the teachings of Muhammad. Muslims believe that God spoke to Muhammad. Their holy book is the Koran, which was first written in Arabic. They believe it is the word of Allah, or "God" in Arabic. A Muslim place of worship is called a mosque.

Muslims have five duties, called the "Pillars of Islam." These duties include five daily prayers, fasting, and making a pilgrimage to Mecca, the birthplace of Muhammad, at least once in a lifetime.

Muslim extremists, including terrorists, have often used the teachings of Islam to justify their actions. Moderate Muslims, however, insist that the teachings of Islam are often misinterpreted, and that their religion does not condone killing or other violence.

For thousands of years, this region was at the crossroads of several trading routes. Camel caravans carried goods between eastern Asia and places in Europe and Africa. With the flow of traffic, Arab settlements along these routes thrived.

Different Religions

Three world religions began in the Middle East: Judaism, Christianity, and Islam. Islam was established on the Arabian Peninsula in the seventh century, and it eventually spread throughout much of the Middle East. The historic region of Palestine is important to followers of all three religions. Some people refer to it as the Holy Land.

Not all Arabs became Muslims. Some Christian Arabs, for example, lived in Mount Lebanon, in what is now Lebanon. Islam never really spread to this mountainous area, which was rugged and hard to reach. Most Arabs who lived there remained Christians.

▼ Muslims at a mosque in Mecca, in Saudi Arabia. Mecca is the birthplace of Muhammad.

Ottoman Rule

In the sixteenth century, the Ottoman Turks conquered much of the Middle East, including Greater Syria. They ruled for about four hundred years, adding to the rich Arab culture. Arab weavers became famous for their beautiful carpets and fabrics, and Arab craftspeople created jewelry

▲ This illustration shows a farm in Greater Syria in the nineteenth century.

boxes inlaid with mother-of-pearl, as well as fine knives and swords. Buildings often featured mosaics, which are intricate patterns of small tiles or stones.

By the 1800s, the Ottoman Empire was in decline. The Ottomans struggled to put down rebellions on the fringes of their empire, and they also feared invasion by the armies of Austria-Hungary and Russia. They took young men from Greater Syria for their armies. In addition, they demanded heavy taxes from the Arabs. Many Arab farmers had a limited amount of land, and they struggled to feed their families. The Ottomans gradually lost control in Greater Syria. Local leaders competed for power, and petty crimes sometimes went unpunished.

In 1869, the Suez Canal opened. This canal linked the Mediterranean and Red Seas, making it easier to ship goods by water than by land routes through Greater Syria. Small businesses along these routes lost income. Silk farmers and weavers were especially hard hit, because silk from the Far East was cheaper than what the Arabs made. This economic decline became a "push" factor for emigration.

Christian Arabs

For the most part, followers of different religions lived peacefully under the rule of the Muslim Ottomans. Christian Arabs, however, were sometimes the targets of persecution. A religious group known as the Druzes resented the Christian Arabs who controlled much of Mount Lebanon. In 1860, Druzes massacred more than seven thousand Christian Arabs. The incident left its mark on Christians in the area, who eventually made up most of the first wave of immigrants to the United States.

American missionaries also had an impact on Christian Arabs. The missionaries first came to Greater Syria in the 1820s, hoping to convert Muslims to Christianity. They did not have much success, but they did create a bond with the region's Christians. Their positive influence became another "push" factor for Arab emigration.

War and Change

World War I resulted in terrible hardship for Greater Syria. The Ottomans sided with the Germans, so Britain and France blockaded seaports in the region. No food could come in, yet the Ottoman rulers demanded more of it to feed their armies. It has been estimated that more than one hundred thousand people from the area around Mount Lebanon died from starvation and disease. After the war ended, in 1918, many Arabs emigrated to the United States to escape the harsh conditions.

The war brought an end to the Ottoman Empire. Britain and France then took control of Greater Syria and other parts of the Middle East. These two countries were slow to allow independence for the region's Arabs. Although Egypt became independent in 1922, British troops remained there until 1956. Iraq became independent in 1933. Syria and Lebanon did not become independent countries until 1946, after World War II had ended. Jordan also became fully independent that year.

Arab-Israeli Conflict

After World War II, the campaign began for an independent Jewish nation in Palestine—which many Jews considered their ancient homeland. Jews had already settled in the region for decades.

Because millions of Jews and others died during the Holocaust, the United States and other countries supported a Jewish nation. Many Arabs in Palestine opposed the idea. By 1948, tensions between Arabs

◀ A tire burns as violence erupts between Palestinians and Israeli soldiers in 2000.

and Jews rose, and the United Nations (UN) created a plan to divide Palestine into separate Jewish and Arab nations. The Arabs rejected this plan, but the Jews accepted it and declared part of Palestine the new nation of Israel.

The birth of Israel enraged many Arabs in the Middle East, and five Arab nations immediately attacked it. Israel won this conflict, gaining more land in Palestine. About 750,000 Arabs fled the region for neighboring Arab countries, and many had to live in refugee camps.

In the following decades, Israel fought more conflicts with Arab nations. After the Six-Day War of 1967, Israel gained control over other parts of the region that was once Palestine. These areas, which include the West Bank and Gaza Strip, have long suffered from poverty and other problems. Arabs living there still have no nation of their own. Many Palestinian Arabs have immigrated to the United States.

⬆ The aftermath of a bombing in Beirut, Lebanon, in 1989. The bombing killed an important Lebanese leader, as well as many other people.

Many Countries, Many Problems

Since the end of World War II, the Middle East has often been a place of turmoil. There has been much conflict, and not just over Palestine. Civil war erupted in Yemen in the 1960s and in Lebanon in the 1970s. In the 1980s, the Iraqi dictator Saddam Hussein led his country into a long, costly war with Iran. His invasion of Kuwait resulted in the Persian Gulf War, in 1991. Hussein was ousted by U.S.-led forces in 2003, during the Iraq War, but those forces still occupy the country.

Some Arab countries, such as Syria and Egypt, have had authoritarian governments that allow few personal freedoms for their citizens. Many Arab countries have suffered from widespread unemployment and poverty.

For some Arabs, the problems they faced pushed them to leave home. Many sought to make new lives in the United States.

CHAPTER 2

Leaving the Middle East

The first wave of Arab immigration began in the late 1870s and lasted until 1924, when the U.S. government established strict new limits on immigration. During this first wave, at least two hundred thousand Arabs emigrated to the United States. About 90 percent of the Arabs who emigrated in the first twenty years were Christians from present-day Lebanon, in the region that was then called Greater Syria. In the United States, these early immigrants were usually known as "Syrians," not Arabs.

Land of Opportunity

The Philadelphia Exposition of 1876 helped start the first wave of Arab emigration. The city of Philadelphia, Pennsylvania, invited merchants from all over the world to sell their wares at a centennial

▼ At the 1876 Philadelphia Exposition, many Americans bought goods sold by Arab traders. Back home, news of their success sparked interest in the United States.

celebration. Traders from Greater Syria brought handcrafted religious items, such as crosses and rosaries. The traders had great success selling these items.

Many Arabs were eager to sell more goods in the United States. They did not intend to settle permanently. Instead, they wanted to earn a lot of money in the United States and then eventually return home.

In the Christian villages in Mount Lebanon, some Arabs were open to the challenge. They were mostly young men, poor and uneducated. By 1887, about two hundred Christian Arabs had left for the United States. A few hundred more followed the next year. By the late 1890s, more than four thousand people were leaving annually. Large families might pool money to send one or two young men. Sometimes, a whole village sponsored travelers.

A Long, Hard Journey

For these emigrants, getting to the United States was not easy. They did not take much with them, though most brought along their cup-shaped hats, called fezzes. Traveling on foot or by donkey, they went to nearby harbor cities, such as Beirut and Tripoli (in modern-day Lebanon), where they got passports and tickets for ships. Officials often demanded bribes in order to let them go on their way.

The ships were usually filthy and over-crowded. Many Arabs traveled on ships that also carried freight, and they might share space with cattle or other livestock.

"Our quarters were cramped beyond imagination . . . The food was the world's worst. The filth was knee-deep. [My two cousins and I] roomed with one other person and a large variety of animal life . . . [My cousin] had his fingernails and toe-nails chewed almost off by the rats."

An Arab immigrant describing his trip to the United States in 1906

Growing Numbers

Despite the difficult journey, the number of Arabs leaving Greater Syria grew. Sometimes, two hundred travelers might leave from the same village. Ottoman rulers became concerned about losing so many taxpayers and potential army recruits. By the 1890s, government officials were stationed at harbor cities and on the roads leading to them. They demanded that Arabs leaving Greater Syria post a bond. If the travelers did not return, they lost their money.

Many Arabs, however, found back roads to the harbor cities, or they paid the bond and let the Ottomans keep the money. If they were caught and sent back, they sought new ways to leave.

After World War I, even larger numbers of Arabs left Greater Syria for the United States. This emigration largely ended in 1924, with the passage of U.S. laws that limited how many Arabs could enter the country.

Other Emigrants

During the early years of emigration, most travelers were men, but a few women also emigrated. Most were wives traveling with their husbands, but some were adventurous single women who traveled

alone. They were making a huge break with tradition—most Arab men believed women needed constant protection.

More Arab women eventually traveled to the United States. Some were wives who went to join their husbands. Others went to marry men who had already emigrated from their villages. In many cases, they had never met their future husbands.

By 1900, a few Muslim men had also left Greater Syria. They were even more determined than Christians to stay in the United

◀ An Arab bride from Greater Syria in the early 1900s. Some Arab women left for the United States to marry men they had never met.

14

States temporarily, and they seldom brought their wives. For them, the United States seemed particularly alien and unknown, since it was a mostly Christian nation with few Muslims.

The Second Wave

A second wave of Arab immigration began in the 1940s, after World War II. Since it began, eight hundred thousand Arabs have emigrated to the United States. The number of Arab emigrants increased dramatically after 1965, when the U.S. government loosened its immigration laws.

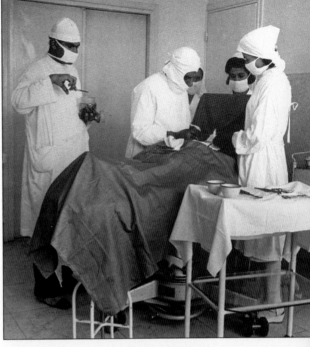

▲ An Arab doctor performs surgery. After World War II, doctors and other professionals left the Middle East to live in the United States.

Travel was easier for this second wave of Arabs, who often went by plane instead of boat. This second wave was different in other ways, too. Arabs now left from many places in the Middle East. Most of them were Muslim, not Christian. Some Arabs left to find better economic opportunities, just like earlier emigrants. Others, however, were escaping conflicts in their homelands or seeking greater personal freedoms. The first Arab-Israeli conflict resulted in many Palestinian refugees, and some eventually made their way to the United States. After the 1967 Arab-Israeli conflict, larger numbers of Arabs left Palestine. Many Arabs escaped from civil wars in Yemen and Lebanon. In Iraq, they fled Saddam Hussein's harsh rule and the long war with Iran. The actions of authoritarian governments in Egypt, Jordan, and Syria caused many Arabs to leave these countries, too.

Unlike earlier emigrants, many of these Arabs were well-educated professionals. For some of them, the problem was not getting to the United States, but leaving their homelands in the first place. Their governments often did not want to lose such highly skilled workers. Some fled their homelands with little planning. Others attended universities in the United States and then simply never went home. This second wave of immigration has sometimes been called the "brain drain," because the Arab world lost so many educated, skilled workers.

CHAPTER **3**

Arriving in the United States

The first wave of Arab immigrants mostly entered the United States through New York City. Some Arabs arrived in other port cities, such as Boston, Massachusetts; and New Orleans, Louisiana. A few also slipped across the Mexican or Canadian borders to enter the country illegally.

Ellis Island
Most Arabs heading into New York City had to stop at Ellis Island, in New York Harbor. The U.S. government had built facilities on the island to screen the flood of immigrants coming into the country by the late 1800s. Facilities on Ellis Island opened in 1892. By the time the government stopped using these facilities, in 1954, more than seventeen million immigrants had passed through the island.

◀ An Algerian immigrant on Ellis Island in the early 1900s.

Help for New Arrivals

In the mid-1890s, the Bureau of Immigration hired an Arabic translator named Najib Arbeely to work at Ellis Island. For many years, Arbeely answered the questions of newly arrived Arabs and helped them through the immigration process. He made sure newcomers got on the right trains and put them in touch with Arab church groups. In addition, he told them about places to find work and where they might find other immigrants who had come from their particular home villages.

In 1892, Najib and his brother, Ibrahim, founded the first Arabic newspaper in the United States, *Kawkab Amika*, or "Star of America."

Like other immigrants, Arabs were dropped off at a large, castle-like building on the island. There, they faced a long, grueling inspection process, conducted in a language they probably did not understand.

U.S. officials checked the health of all immigrants. An eye infection called trachoma kept the greatest number of immigrants from being admitted. Arabs with trachoma or some other contagious ailment might be sent back on the boat that had just brought them. Or, they might have to wait in a hospital on Ellis Island until they were well.

Besides being healthy, immigrants also had to have money in their pockets. Officials asked them what city they were traveling to, if they had tickets for the trip, and if they had jobs waiting. Officials might also change an immigrant's name to something that was easier to write and say, and which sounded to them more "American." When the officials were satisfied with the answers to all their questions, the immigrants could go. The whole process took between three to five hours.

New York and Beyond

In the early 1900s, many Arab newcomers settled immediately in New York City, which had a thriving Arab community. There, newcomers found other people from their villages back home, who could help them get jobs and housing. Many Arabs stayed in the city or its surrounding areas for the rest of their lives.

"It was just near Christmastime, the lights were all lit . . . I looked in these store windows until I was flabbergasted . . . We didn't know what to do with the toilet. . . . We argued whether to wash in it or drink from it. We finally decided it was to wash our feet in, so we did."

An Arab woman describing her impressions of
Hartford City, Indiana, as a young girl in the early 1900s

Some Arabs traveled to other cities before settling. Many took trains to cities such as Boston and Philadelphia.

Other newcomers traveled much farther. By 1910, Arab peddlers could be found in most parts of the United States, with supply networks established around the country. After selling door to door for a while, experienced peddlers often settled in a particular area, creating a supply station there. Then, they recruited peddlers from

The Syrian Ladies Aid Society

In 1907, twelve Arab women from New York City, who had arrived earlier with their husbands, formed an organization called the Syrian Ladies Aid Society. It provided "financial, medical, and moral aid" to Syrian women and girls arriving at Ellis Island. A woman working for the group would be stationed on the island, and she would offer to help the newly arrived find work, housing, and relatives from home.

A similar society was formed in Boston in 1917, though it was originally created to help people in Greater Syria who had suffered through World War I. Later, it also helped poor Arabs in Boston get food, coal for heating, and money for rent.

▲ Members of the Syrian Ladies Aid Society at a celebration of its fiftieth anniversary, in 1958.

their villages back home. Newly arrived Arabs went directly to the settlement that had developed around the supplier, which served as a home base for traveling peddlers. Newcomers received products to sell, and they went right to work. They often banked their money at the settlement, and they even received their mail there, too.

▲ Immigrants on Ellis Island in the early 1900s. The men are wearing fezzes. At that time, many Arab men wore these stiff, cup-shaped hats.

Early Muslim Arrivals

Muslims only made up about 10 percent of the first wave of Arab immigration. Some Syrian Muslims became peddlers. Others claimed free land under the Homestead Act of 1862, moving to places such as North Dakota and Iowa to become farmers.

Most of the early Muslim immigrants, however, went to large cities, where they could find factory jobs in heavy industries. They went to Detroit and Dearborn in Michigan, to work in car factories. They went to Pittsburgh or New Castle in Pennsylvania, to labor in steel mills. They also went to factory jobs in Peoria, Illinois, and Michigan City, Indiana.

In these cities, newly arrived Muslim Arabs settled in tight-knit Muslim communities. They could find other people from their home villages in these communities, and they could also maintain their religion and some of the familiar traditions of their homeland.

Arabs and Citizenship

Although most early Arab immigrants planned to return home some day, many became U.S. citizens. Arabs who had legally entered the United States were resident aliens who had most of the same rights as Americans. After living in the country for five years, they could apply for citizenship. They were required to swear allegiance to the United States and, after 1906, also to speak English.

In the early twentieth century, some Arabs had trouble becoming citizens. At the time, U.S. immigration laws excluded certain races from citizenship, such as Asians. Some U.S. officials began denying Arab requests for citizenship, on the grounds that Arabs were actually Asian. The U.S. government eventually decided that Arabs were in fact "white." Still, these problems reflected the ignorance and racism that Arabs often faced.

▲ An Egyptian immigrant holds his son during a swearing-in ceremony for new U.S. citizens.

Second Wave Arrivals

Arriving in the United States was much different for the second wave of Arab immigrants. Most immigrants came by plane, not boat, and they had approval to stay in the United States before they left home. The process of entering the country was much easier for them.

In 1965, the United States changed its immigration laws. The changes had a big impact on Arab immigration. For years, entry to the United States depended on a person's race and home country. After 1965, U.S. immigration officials focused on reuniting families, bringing in skilled workers, and providing a haven for refugees. Many Arabs were sponsored by relatives who had already become U.S. citizens. Others entered the country as skilled professionals or refugees from various conflicts. Arab students also arrived to attend U.S. universities.

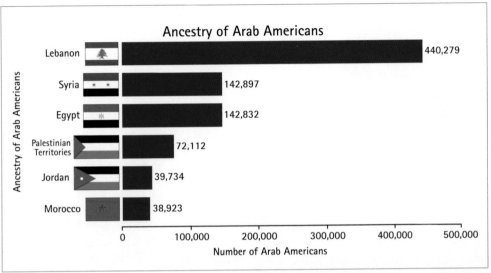

Source: U.S. Census Bureau, Census 2000

▲ This chart shows the top six countries that Arab Americans claim as the homeland of their ancestors.

By the late 1960s, Arabs from many countries in the Middle East were arriving in the United States in large numbers. Most were Muslim, but some were Christians from Lebanon and Iraq. Many went to large cities with established Arab communities, such as the Detroit area, Chicago, and New York City. They also went to cities in California, such as Los Angeles. New arrivals tended to settle in cities where they could join other people from their particular homeland. Many Iraqis and Palestinians went to live in the Detroit area. A large number of Egyptians settled in Jersey City, New Jersey, and Washington, D.C. Yemenis settled in Detroit or went to farms in California. Many Arabs went to live in Texas.

Education and income also affected where Arabs settled. Former students might settle in the places where they had gone to school, and many professionals also settled in places that had large universities.

"Customs and immigrations officials were cordial. Sean [an American friend] sped through formalities while I waited for officials to search my bags [and] fingerprint me. . . . I signed where I was told to sign. . . . Moments later I was directed to the passport checkpoint, where I was greeted by a middle aged woman who asked me to consider changing my name to a more suitable American name."

Jamil I. Toubbeh, Palestinian, remembering his arrival in the United States in 1951

Early History of Arab Immigration

CHAPTER 4

For the most part, early Arab immigrants came to the United States to make a lot of money quickly. They planned to return home and use the money to create better lives for their families. A large number had been farmers in their homeland. In the United States, many chose to make their fortunes as peddlers. Peddling did not require a lot of training or even a good command of English. Most Arabs were also attracted to the idea of being their own bosses.

At first, many Arabs joined the ranks of pushcart peddlers in New York City and other large cities on the East Coast. By the mid-1890s, new arrivals were fanning out into small towns and rural areas, where there was less competition.

Working on the Road

Peddling was a hard life. Carrying heavy backpacks, peddlers walked hundreds of miles in all kinds of weather. They often had no idea where they would sleep or find a meal. Most immigrants knew very little English and could not read and write in their native Arabic. Not knowing the language or the customs of Americans, they sometimes got in trouble. Arab peddlers were beaten, robbed, and even killed. Surprisingly, given the conditions, many peddlers were women.

Yet for all its drawbacks, peddling offered many benefits. Peddlers had to learn English to survive. Traveling from home to home, they also learned a lot about the United States. Their main customers were housewives, and they carried everything a house-wife might want or need: rosaries and other religious items, but also clothing, household items, and costume jewelry. Through hard work and ingenuity, many of these peddlers realized their goals. By 1910, Arab peddlers earned three times the average annual income of American workers.

▲ For Arab peddlers in the United States, a horse and carriage made life much easier.

"My father . . . migrated to this country from Lebanon in 1899 . . . He began back peddling. . . . His pack consisted of dry goods, mostly cut yardage, and clothing, shirts, work clothing, socks, pants, and underwear. . . The pack was supported by a strap which went over the shoulder, and although the strap was rather wide, it rubbed his shoulder enough to make a calloused place. The callous remained on his shoulder until his death, many years after he quit peddling on foot. In addition to the large back-pack, he carried a hand grip [bag], which held combs, thread, needles, and all such notions that women and men would need, like shaving cream, straight razors . . ."

Abraham Modi, an Arab American from West Virginia

As soon as they could afford to, peddlers bought a horse and carriage for carrying their goods. For some, the next step was getting off the road and becoming a supplier for other peddlers. Suppliers would recruit new peddlers from their home villages, and then small settlements would grow around the supplier. Eventually, supply networks brought goods from the East Coast to places all across the country.

Cities and Towns

Not all Arab immigrants were traveling peddlers. By the turn of the century, about half of Arab immigrants lived in New York City, which had its own Arab community, called "Little Syria."

⬆ A man sells drinks from a container on his back in "Little Syria" in New York City. By the early 1900s, the neighborhood was a thriving Arab community.

The neighborhood was full of coffeehouses, bazaars, and shops. Here, Arab men wearing traditional fezzes played backgammon or smoked tobacco in water pipes, while Arab women in colorful dresses shopped for traditional food in Arab groceries. Drawing on their experience with silk weaving back home, Arabs also established many silk factories in New York and New Jersey.

"Little Syrias" also sprung up in Boston and other cities in the northeast. Some Arabs found work in textile factories in New England. Arabs also went to towns and cities in other parts of the country. They settled in places such as Cedar Rapids, Iowa; Peoria, Illinois; Green Bay, Wisconsin; Vicksburg, Mississippi; and San Francisco, California.

Women and Family

When Arab immigration began, a few single women traveled to the United States, and some wives accompanied their husbands. For the most part, however, early Arab immigrants were men.

Married men could send for their wives and children to join them when they had made enough money. Single men faced a different situation. Many were eager to marry and start families. Since Arab men in the United States greatly outnumbered Arab women, finding an Arab wife could be difficult.

Some men asked relatives in their villages back home to find them brides. Others traveled back home to find a bride and then return to the United States. A small number married non-Arab women. By 1910, one-third of Arab immigrants in the United States were women.

With marriage came families. The family was the center of life for Arab immigrants. Through the family, immigrants maintained their homeland's traditions and values. A man was the head of the household, obeyed by his wife and children. Women raised the children and did household chores. Boys were often valued more than girls, who were expected to stay at home until their parents found them husbands.

"Bachelors value money lightly; they squander it in clubs, theaters . . . All of these places are traps for immigrants in a foreign land. A man who marries and has a family is respected, responsible, and motivated to save . . . mates should be chosen not for their wealth but for their education. Such wives will create enduring happiness."

From an 1899 article in Al-Hoda, *an Arab newspaper in the United States*

From the start, however, life in the United States had an impact on traditional ways. Women gained a certain amount of freedom because they often had to work to support the family. As time passed, many began to push for greater equality. Children were often exposed to a different way of life outside the family, and they also challenged old traditions.

▼ Arab children play on a sidewalk in New York City.

◀ An Arab restaurant in New York City in the 1930s. By then, many Arabs had established their own businesses.

Living as Outsiders

Before World War I, most Arabs in the United States did not consider themselves "American." Arab immigrants called their communities *Al-Nizala*, which means "temporary settlement" in Arabic. Most saw themselves as outsiders who had not put down roots. They took care not to offend "Americans" and not to break any U.S. laws, but they had little contact with non-Arabs. Their first loyalty was to their families and villages back home. Arab-language newspapers also focused on the homeland.

As outsiders, Arabs sometimes faced prejudice. Many Americans did not know much about "Syrians," except that they looked and acted suspiciously foreign. Some Americans considered Arabs to be "parasites," since they sent much of their earnings back home.

Becoming More American

After World War I, the attitudes of Arabs in the United States changed. The war and other factors had devastated their homeland. Large numbers of Arab immigrants were arriving in the United States, not to make their fortunes but to start new lives. Then, in 1924, new U.S. laws cut off immigration from the Middle East. Many Arabs began to realize they were never going home again.

This change in outlook had important consequences. Arabs stopped sending their earnings to the homeland. Instead, they used those earnings to improve their lives in the United States. Peddling had become much less profitable, and many peddlers settled down by opening their own family businesses, such as grocery stores. Others found work in factories. Many Arabs moved from the cramped conditions of the inner city to nicer places outside of cities. They put more emphasis on their children's educations, since these children would be the key to future success for their families.

In short, Arabs became more a part of American society. They left

"That first generation of the immigrant Arabs really wanted to be 100 percent American and changed their names and their religions even. . . . And so when you're raised in that kind of atmosphere, you wanted to be an all-American. Yet . . . I've found in going back to Syria or Lebanon, through the food, the atmosphere, the air, the sights, sound, you feel a root . . . It just is down inside you."

*Najeeb Halaby,
an Arab American who became
a U.S. government official and
business leader*

▲ A 1938 portrait of Salloum Mokarzel, founder of the Arab American newspaper *The Syrian World*, with his wife and daughters. The newspaper was published in English rather than Arabic. After World War I, Arabs began adopting more American lifestyles.

Arab Christianity

Arab immigrants from Greater Syria practiced a different kind of Christianity than Roman Catholics and Protestants. They belonged to either the Orthodox or Eastern Rite Church. Many traditions and practices of these churches developed in the Middle East long ago.

When Christian Arabs first came to the United States, they attended Roman Catholic churches. As their communities grew, they established their own churches, in New York City and other places.

As Arabs became more American, their religious practices changed, too. Arabs began marrying people of other Christian faiths. Their churches often abandoned some of the old traditions, further breaking ties to the homeland.

behind many of their old customs. They got involved in U.S. politics. More Arab men began to marry non-Arab women. Like their fellow Americans, Arabs struggled through the Great Depression of the 1930s, and many fought in World War II. As Arabs became more successful, they entered the middle class, buying new houses, cars, and appliances. Later generations spoke English instead of Arabic, and they adopted American customs and dress. They also went to college, and many became professionals.

Becoming American brought stability and comfort, but it came at a price. Later generations often knew little of their Arabic heritage. In many cases, they downplayed their Arab ancestry.

Muslim Immigrants

A small number of Muslims arrived in the first wave of Arab immigrants. Like Christian Arabs, they were mostly male, and they were poor and uneducated. Some became peddlers, but many Muslims did not feel comfortable going into Christians' homes. Instead, they went to large cities and took factory jobs, where they could earn steady paychecks. Beginning in about 1914, many took jobs in the Detroit area, at the factories of Ford and other auto companies.

In many ways, daily life in the United States presented challenges for Muslims. Their day of worship was on Friday, not Sunday. They had to pray five times a day, which could be difficult or impossible when working. They also had to fast. Yet many Muslims managed to adapt their religious practices to their new

▲ Arab American James Jabara, shown here in 1953, was a top fighter pilot during World War II and the Korean War.

lives. They changed their day of worship to Sunday, and they said their prayers after their work shifts had ended. Though it was hard, they fasted during their workdays. Few mosques were built in the United States before World War II, but Muslims could pray together in homes and other places.

Like Christian Arabs, most Muslim men were without wives at first. Married men eventually sent for their wives, and single men often traveled back home to find a bride. Some Muslim men married non-Muslim women in the United States.

In the decades after their first arrival, Muslim Arabs became more American, just like Christian Arabs. More of them married non-Muslims. Later generations could not speak Arabic. As time passed, the heritage of the homeland faded.

Recent History of Arab Americans

After World War II ended, Arabs began entering the United States again. They came from a variety of countries in the Middle East, and quite a few were escaping turmoil in their homelands. Many were refugees who fled Palestine after the birth of Israel.

Most of these immigrants were men, just like earlier immigrants. In other ways, however, these Arabs were different from earlier arrivals. Most of them were Muslim, and many were professionals, such as doctors, teachers, and engineers. These professionals were not poor. They were well educated and often fluent in English, and they were able to find high-paying jobs in the United States. Some were students who attended U.S. universities and then decided to stay because there were no jobs back home.

These immigrants were different in other ways, too. For many, going home was not an option, so they had to build new lives in the United States. Some went to established Arab communities in places such as Detroit, but others were spread across the country. They often had little contact with first-wave Arab immigrants. Many downplayed their Arab and Muslim identities. They were less committed to the daily practices of Islam, and a large number married non-Muslims.

Changing Attitudes

The year 1967 is important in the history of Arab Americans. In June of that year, Israel fought a conflict with other Arab countries called the Six-Day War. In just six days, Israel crushed Egyptian, Syrian, and Jordanian forces. It also took control of the Palestinian territories outside of Israel, where many Arabs lived. Israeli troops began an occupation of these territories that continues to this day.

▶ Israeli soldiers guard Egyptian prisoners during the 1967 Six-Day War.

Like other Arabs in the world, Arabs in the United States were devastated by this turn of events. Just as devastating for them, however, was the U.S. reaction. Israel was an important U.S. ally, and most Americans cheered the Israeli victory. Arab Americans had long understood the close relationship between Israel and the United States. After World War II, a few Arab Americans had tried to influence U.S. policy toward Palestine and the birth of Israel, without success. Still, U.S. attitudes toward the 1967 conflict shocked Arab Americans, both Christian and Muslim alike. They believed that the U.S. view of the conflict was unfairly one-sided and pro-Israel, especially in the media.

This conflict had a huge effect on Arab Americans. For decades, Arabs had been leaving their old heritage behind as they became part of U.S. society. Now, however, Arab Americans rediscovered their heritage. They had a new sense of pride in being Arab. Some began questioning how "American" they had become. At the same time, Arabs became more politically active. They began forming groups that sought to influence U.S. policy in the Middle East and change how Arabs were viewed in the United States.

> "After 1967 and the tremendous loss then, I concentrated on the Palestinian cause and Arabism; I made . . . [fewer] American friends."
>
> *An Arab American in Detroit*

A New Wave of Immigrants

In the late 1960s, a greater number of Arabs began arriving in the United States. They have sometimes been called the third wave of Arab immigration. Many came from Israeli-occupied territories. Others came from Lebanon, Syria, Jordan, Egypt, Iraq, and Yemen. This wave has continued into the twenty-first century.

These volunteers are encouraging Arab Americans to register to vote.

Arab American Groups

One effect of the 1967 Six-Day War was the formation of new Arab American groups. The first group was the Association of Arab-American University Graduates (AAUG), which formed in late 1967. It sought to educate people about the Arab world and influence U.S. lawmakers. It also tried to get more Arab Americans to become politically active.

After the AAUG, other groups formed, such as the National Association of Arab Americans (NAAA) and the American-Arab Anti-Discrimination Committee (ADC). Today, Arab American groups continue their efforts to advance the cause of Arabs.

Like the Arabs who first arrived after World War II, most of these immigrants were Muslim, though Christians did arrive from Iraq and Lebanon. Many were students or professionals, though uneducated immigrants also arrived. Again, many of the immigrants were men, but women arrived, too. These women mostly came with their families or to join relatives already living in the United States.

Growing Arab Communities

Most of these Arabs settled in Arab communities in large cities, often with the help of relatives who had arrived earlier. Through the years, the communities grew. Mosques were built and Muslim schools were established. Various organizations were created to provide resources for Arabs. In their communities, Arabs could find the food, music, art, and literature of their homelands.

For these later immigrants, keeping alive their Arab culture was very important. Muslims put a strong emphasis on practicing Islam. They often relied upon institutions in their communities, such as mosques and schools. Many of these Arabs disapproved of U.S. culture, which they considered too secular and permissive. They also believed that earlier Arab generations had become too American in their behavior and practices. Unlike the earlier wave of immigrants after World

▶ Many neighborhoods in the Detroit/Dearborn area show a strong Arab influence.

War II, they tended to marry other Muslims. They strongly disagreed with U.S. policy in the Middle East, especially toward Israel and the situation in Palestine.

At the same time, however, these later immigrants were eager to take advantage of what the United States had to offer. They put down roots and helped their communities grow. Many pursued more education. They worked hard at their jobs, too. Some found skilled professional jobs. Others worked in factories or found jobs in the service industry, such as in restaurants. Like earlier Arab immigrants, some started their own businesses. Many worked as managers and salespeople. Arabs participated in democracy, too, with many becoming active in the Arab-American political groups that sprang up after the Six-Day War of 1967.

An Arab "Capital"

Detroit has sometimes been called the Arab "capital" of the United States. An estimated two hundred thousand people of Arab descent live in the Detroit area, which includes nearby Dearborn. Many Arabs first settled in the area to work in its car factories. Later, when factory jobs became less plentiful, Arabs still kept arriving, drawn to Detroit's tight-knit Arab neighborhoods. Many went to work in Arab-owned businesses.

Some Arab neighborhoods in the Detroit area seem like separate Arab worlds. People on the street speak Arabic. Street signs and store signs are in both Arabic and English. There are Arab mosques and schools, as well as dozens of Arab businesses. People read Arab-language newspapers, and they can choose from Arab radio and television programs. Some public schools even provide bilingual instruction in both Arabic and English.

▲ Muslims in Virginia shop before the start of Ramadan. During Ramadan, the meal after a day of fasting is often a time for family and friends to come together.

Muslim Holidays

In the United States, Muslim Arabs observe the same religious holidays as other Muslims around the world. Ramadan is an important time of year. It is a month of fasting and intense prayer. During Ramadan, Muslims cannot eat or drink any- thing between sunrise and sunset.

Arabs celebrate the end of Ramadan with *Eid Al-Fitr*. They dress in nice clothes, decorate their homes, and visit with friends and family. Another celebration is *Eid Al-Adha*, which takes place at the end of the *Hajj*, the annual pilgrimage to Mecca. Muslims also celebrate the Islamic New Year and the birthday of Muhammad. Muslim holidays are all based on the Islamic calendar, and they fall on different days each year.

Arab Women in the United States

Life in the United States has sometimes been hardest for Arab women. They can face two challenges. One is their own traditional Arab culture. In this culture, women often do not have much power or freedom, and there are strict limits on how they may lead their lives. The other challenge is the prejudice they may face for how they look and act. Compared to American women, many Arab women tend to dress modestly. Muslim women might wear long, loose clothing. They might also wear a head covering, called a hijab.

Arab women have not all had the same experiences in the United States. More educated women have often enjoyed greater freedom and opportunities. Later generations of first-wave Arabs sometimes have little connection to traditional Arab culture. They look and act like other American women. Some Arab women, however, do live in traditional Arab households, where the man has the final say and the woman's main role is taking care of the family. Yet even these women have often sought out new opportunities in education and jobs. In many cases, the men may struggle to accept the greater freedom that most women have in the United States.

No matter what their backgrounds, Arab women have often been the "glue" that holds together and strengthens Arab communities. They are often responsible for maintaining Arab traditions. In many cases, Arab women have helped create and support schools, mosques, churches, and other important community resources.

"My husband . . . couldn't stand the idea that I was really changing, he will blame anything. It could be school, it could be my American friends, it could be America. 'I brought you to America and now you're a different person.' But he never really understood the underlying issue that 'I am not yours, and I am who I am.'"

Immigrant woman
from Yemen

Wearing the Hijab

In Muslim countries, Muslim women usually wear a head covering called a hijab. The hijab has its roots in the Koran, which instructs women to dress modestly in public, especially in the presence of the opposite sex. There are different kinds of hijabs, and Muslim women wear them in different ways. Some women wear a scarf that covers the head and neck, while others also wear a veil to cover the face, so only the eyes are visible.

Some people think the hijab is repressive for women. In many countries, women must wear a hijab or face strong criticism by others in their communities. Some governments require that a woman wear a hijab. Yet many Muslim women say they prefer to wear one. Some women say it protects them from being harassed by men. Muslim women also wear a hijab as an expression of their Muslim faith.

In the United States, many Arab women wear a hijab. Wearing one, however, has often led to discrimination when looking for jobs or housing. In the workplace, Arab women may be asked to remove their hijabs, and refusing to do so may get them fired. The hijab has also made Arab women easy targets for harassment. In the aftermath of the 9/11 terrorist attacks, many Arab women stopped wearing their hijabs because they feared for their safety.

▲ Students gather outside of Fordson High School in Dearborn, Michigan. The school's student population is 90 percent Arab or Muslim.

New Generations

In recent decades, young Arab Americans have sometimes been torn between the world of their parents and the American life they have experienced outside the home. Although they are proud of their Arab heritage, they also get exposed to U.S. culture, such as clothes, music, and food. At home, tradition is important, and so is the authority of their elders. Outside the home, they learn that Americans prize youth and change, and that many young people have a lot of freedom.

Teenage girls often experience the most problems, especially when it comes to dating. In their families, they may see a double standard: their brothers can do what they please, but they cannot. The men in their families—both fathers and brothers—are often very concerned about the girls' relationships with boys, especially ones who are non-Muslim.

September 11 Attacks

On September 11, 2001, Muslim extremists belonging to the al-Qaeda terrorist network hijacked four U.S. passenger planes. Two planes crashed into the twin towers of New York City's World Trade Center, and both towers then collapsed. A third plane hit the Pentagon near Washington, D.C., and the fourth crashed in a field near Shanksville, Pennsylvania. These attacks resulted in thousands of deaths.

Not all the terrorists were Arabs, and none were Arab-American citizens. Yet the attacks were a huge setback for Arabs in the United States. Most Arabs were horrified and saddened by the attacks. Arab American organizations condemned them, and many Arab groups raised money for the victims. Arab Americans were also among the rescue workers in New York City. Nonetheless, in the days and months after the attacks, the backlash against Arabs was far-reaching and extreme. Many Arabs faced harassment. Homes and mosques were vandalized, and Arabs were beaten and even killed.

Since the attacks, Arabs have often been viewed as potential terrorists, by both their fellow citizens and the government. Some have lost jobs. Others have been investigated and even arrested. The government now has broad powers to combat terrorism, and law enforcement officials have often focused their attention on Arabs. In some cases, Arabs have been arrested without even knowing the charges brought against them.

"A couple of days after September 11, my brother . . . was jumped by a group of guys just chanting . . . and he had his lip split open, and they bashed the wind- shield of his car with a beer bottle."

An Arab woman in the United States

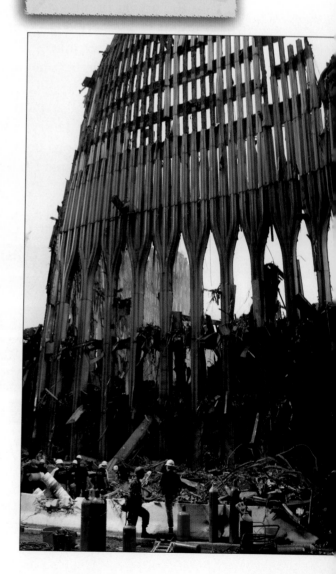

▶ Workers at the site of the World Trade Center after the 9/11 terrorist attacks. The attacks caused an incredible amount of destruction and killed thousands of people.

Arab Americans in U.S. Society

In the 2000 U.S. Census, 1.2 million Americans claimed some kind of Arab ancestry. Many Arab American organizations insist that the actual number is higher—as much as three million. These numbers are still small compared to the millions of people from Europe and other places that have immigrated to the United States. Yet Arabs have become an important part of communities all across the country.

About half of all Arab Americans live in the states of California, Florida, Michigan, New Jersey, and New York. Most live in urban areas. The Detroit/Dearborn area has one of the highest concentrations of Arabs in the United States.

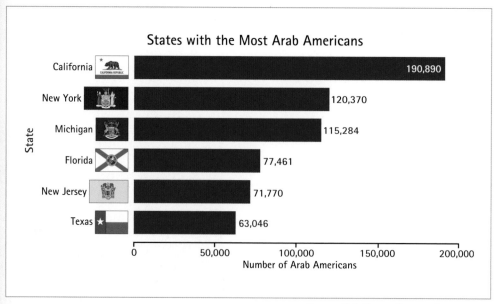

States with the Most Arab Americans

State	Number of Arab Americans
California	190,890
New York	120,370
Michigan	115,284
Florida	77,461
New Jersey	71,770
Texas	63,046

Source: U.S. Census Bureau, Census 2000

▲ This charts shows the top six states with the largest Arab populations.

Arab Food

Through the years, Arab restaurants have introduced Americans to different kinds of Arab food, particularly Lebanese dishes. Today, Americans are familiar with many Arab foods, such as tabbouleh (a salad that includes cracked wheat, parsley, mint, and lemon), hummus (mashed chickpeas), pita bread, shish kebab (marinated meat on skewers), and sherbet (*sharbaat* in Arabic).

An Arab may have had a hand in creating an American favorite—the ice cream cone. At the 1904 St. Louis World's Fair, an Arab immigrant is said to have put ice cream in a rolled-up Arab pastry, called zalabia, after containers for ice cream had run out. Although we may never know who invented the ice cream cone, historians agree that it first became popular at the St. Louis World's Fair.

▲ A woman makes bread during the annual Arab International Festival in Dearborn.

Arab Americans come from a variety of different backgrounds. Many have roots in the former region of Greater Syria, with almost 40 percent claiming Lebanese ancestry and almost 12 percent claiming Syrian roots. Another 12 percent have ancestry in Egypt. The rest claim roots in a variety of other places in the Middle East.

Education and Work

Despite the many obstacles they have faced, Arabs have prospered in the United States. The number of Arab Americans who have gone to college is higher than the national average. The average household income of Arab Americans is also higher than Americans as a whole.

Since the early days of backpack peddlers, many Arab Americans have preferred to be their own bosses. Compared to other immigrant groups, Arabs have a high percentage of entrepreneurs. Many own small businesses, such as stores and restaurants, but there have been larger success stories. In the 1920s, Joseph Haggar created a line of men's clothing that is still popular today. More recently, Paul Orfalea created the Kinko's chain of copy centers.

Many other Arabs are highly skilled professionals. They have pursued successful careers in finance, banking, law, and science.

◀ Playing for the New England Patriots, Doug Flutie throws a pass.

Contributions of Arab Americans

Arab Americans have made a big impact on American life in many areas. Cardiac surgeon Michael DeBakey became famous for pioneering life-saving techniques in heart operations. Two Arab Americans have won Nobel Prizes for their work in science. Arab Americans have also made their mark in the entertainment industry. Danny Thomas was an early star of television. Singer Paul Anka had several pop hits in the 1950s and 1960s, and Frank Zappa was an important rock-music pioneer. Paula Abdul has been successful as a choreographer, dancer, and singer. Well-known Hollywood actors include F. Murray Abraham and Tony Shalhoub. Some Arab Americans have been successful athletes, such as NFL quarterback Doug Flutie.

Arab Americans have also played important roles in politics. Several have served in the U.S. Congress, including former Senate majority leader George Mitchell. In 2000, Ralph Nader, a long-time champion of consumer rights and the environment, ran for U.S. president. John Henry Sununu was governor of New Hampshire and served as Chief of Staff for U.S. president George H. W. Bush. Donna Shalala was head of the U.S. Department of Health and Human Services under President Bill Clinton.

St. Jude Hospital

Danny Thomas (1914–1991) was born and raised in Detroit, the son of Lebanese Christian immigrants. He became a hugely popular television star. In 1962, Thomas established St. Jude Children's Research Hospital, in Memphis, Tennessee. The hospital conducts research on cancer and other illnesses, and it also provides care to sick children. It never turns away patients who cannot pay.

Speaking about the hospital, Thomas said: "I thought of the hundreds of thousands of people of my heritage who had come to America. They had prospered, they had educated their children, and they had passed on. They had made individual contributions to society, but they had never united in a common cause all their own. Maybe St. Jude Children's Research Hospital could become their common cause."

▲ Danny Thomas in 1965. A star on television in the 1950s and 1960s, he founded St. Jude Hospital.

Confronting Problems

Despite their many accomplishments, Arab Americans continue to face difficulties. One problem is the stereotypes of Arabs held by some Americans. They think Arabs are a backwards people, rigid in their beliefs and prone to violence. In some Hollywood movies, the "bad guys" have been Arabs.

Prejudice toward Arabs has often been sparked by specific events. During the Persian Gulf War, some Arabs in the United States were the victims of hate crimes. After the Oklahoma City bombings and other terrorist acts in the 1990s, the U.S. government enacted new antiterrorism measures, which often targeted Arabs. The violence caused by Palestinian suicide bombers has also affected many Americans' perceptions, and so has the war in Iraq.

The 9/11 attacks have had the most dramatic impact on the lives of Arab Americans. These attacks, however, have also been a wake-up call. Many Arabs now realize that they must work harder to educate other Americans about what it means to be an Arab.

> "I'm glad I look like a terrorist because it gives me a special sword to help destroy the stereotype that continues to injure my people, distort our image and to cause otherwise compassionate Americans to engage in hateful acts of bias . . . Humor can provide an excellent medium to break down the barriers that prevent people from understanding each other."
>
> *Ray Hanania, Arab*
> *American writer*
> *and comedian*

Like other immigrant groups, Arabs in the United States often feel torn between becoming more American and keeping the heritage of their homeland. Later generations of the first Arab immigrants have often lost touch with much of their Arab culture. Among more recent waves of immigrants, many have questioned how far Arabs should go in adapting to the American way of life. Many Arab Americans feel they have lost much of their Arab identity but are still not accepted by their fellow Americans.

Looking to the Future

Arab Americans have made a lot of progress toward building better lives in the United States. Some have sought to expose people to

Celebrating the Arab World

Some Arabs in the United States have sought to focus attention on Arab culture. The Palestinian Heritage Foundation, for example, has created exhibits that showcase different aspects of Palestinian culture, while the Near Eastern Music Ensemble plays various kinds of Arab music. Novelist Diana Abu-Jaber has written novels about the conflict between Arab and American cultures.

In May 2005, the Arab American National Museum opened in Dearborn, Michigan. The museum tells the story of Arab immigrants and highlights the accomplishments of Arab Americans. It has more than five hundred exhibits.

On the museum's opening day, Arab American actor Tony Shalhoub said, "So much has been said about us that is not accurate, that's wrong or worse. The Arab American National Museum is where our story can be told accurately and fully."

▲ Opening day for the Arab American National Museum.

the music, dance, and literature of Arab culture. Others have tried to explain Arab culture to non-Arabs. Muslim Arabs have had success in getting businesses to accommodate their religious practices. At the same time, American culture has benefited Arabs in many ways. Arab women, for example, have often enjoyed greater personal freedom.

Since the first days of Arab immigration, Arab Americans have proven themselves to be a hard-working and resourceful people, always eager for new opportunities. There is no doubt that they will meet the fresh challenges of tomorrow.

Notable Arab Americans

Farouk el Baz (1938–) Egyptian-born scientist who was a pioneer in the use of space photography. He helped train astronauts who landed on the Moon.

Jamie Farr (1936–) U.S.-born actor who played Corporal Klinger in the popular television series *Mash* in the 1970s and 1980s.

Kahlil Gibran (1883–1931) Lebanese-born writer who is most famous for the popular book *The Prophet* (1923).

Najeeb Halaby (1915–2003) U.S.-born business leader and government official who headed the Federal Aviation Administration (FAA) in the 1960s. His daughter is Lisa Halaby, who married Jordan's King Hussein and became Queen Noor of Jordan.

Raymond G. Hanania (1953–) U.S.-born journalist, author, and stand-up comedian who has focused on the problems faced by Arab Americans.

James Jabara (1923–1966) U.S.-born fighter pilot who was highly decorated for his service during World War II and the Korean War.

Casey Kasem (1932–) U.S.-born radio personality and disk jockey who hosted the *American Top 40* radio program for many years.

Candy Lightner (1946–) U.S.-born founder of Mothers Against Drunk Driving (MADD).

Christa McAuliffe (1948–1986) U.S.-born school teacher who was the first citizen passenger aboard a space flight. She was killed in the *Challenger* space shuttle disaster, in 1986.

George Mitchell (1933–) U.S.-born politician. He was majority leader of the U.S. Senate from 1989 to 1995. After leaving office, he led a fact-finding commission on ways to resolve the Palestinian situation.

Bobby Rahal (1953–) U.S.-born race car driver who won the Indianapolis 500 (1986) and many other races.

Yasser Seirawan (1960–) Syrian-born chess grandmaster who has often represented the United States in international competition.

Tony Shalhoub (1953–) U.S.-born actor who has appeared in movies and television shows, including the television series *Monk*.

Helen Thomas (1920–) U.S.-born journalist. Known as the "First Lady of the Press," she has reported on every U.S. president since John F. Kennedy.

Time Line

1869   Suez Canal opens to shipping.

1876   Philadelphia Exposition takes place; Arab traders participate in the exposition, and their success sparks interest in the United States as a promising new market.

1892   Ellis Island begins processing immigrants.

1918   World War I ends, and the Ottoman Empire falls; the British. and French begin controlling much of the Middle East.

1922   Egypt becomes an independent nation.

1933   Iraq becomes an independent nation.

1924   The Immigration Act of 1924 puts severe limits on the number of Arab immigrants allowed into the United States.

1946   Lebanon and Syria become independent nations.

1948   Israel is established and the first Arab-Israeli conflict begins.

1962   Danny Thomas establishes St. Jude Children's Research Hospital, in Memphis, Tennessee.

1965   Changes to immigration law allow many more Arabs to emigrate to the United States.

1967   Israel wins the Six-Day War and begins occupying Palestinian territories where many Arabs live.

1975   Civil war erupts in Lebanon and lasts for more than fifteen years; assassinations and other violence continue into the twenty-first century.

1980   Conflict between Iraq and Iran begins.

1991   Iraqi forces invade Kuwait; in the Persian Gulf War that follows, UN forces, led by the United States, defeat Iraqi troops and liberate Kuwait.

2001   Al-Qaeda terrorists hijack four passenger planes and crash them into the World Trade Center towers in New York City, the Pentagon, in Washington, D.C., and a field in Pennsylvania.

2003   Forces led by the United States invade Iraq, topple Saddam Hussein's regime, and occupy the country.

2005   The Arab American National Museum opens in Dearborn, Michigan.

Glossary

aliens people living in a nation other than their birth nation who have not become citizens of their new nation of residence

authoritarian having a government in which a single leader or party holds absolute power and individual freedoms are restricted

bond an amount of money that a person agrees to give up if an obligation is not kept

census population count

culture language, beliefs, customs, and ways of life shared by a group of people from the same region or nation

discrimination negative treatment of a certain group of people

emigrate leave one nation or region to go and live in another place

entrepreneurs people who create and run their own businesses, often by taking big risks with their money

extremists people who hold very strong views about politics or religion and believe in extreme action, including violence

fasting not eating or drinking, often for religious reasons

fluent able to speak a language easily and well

hate crimes physical attacks or other crimes that are motivated by prejudice

heritage traditions and customs handed down from previous generations

Holocaust the systematic killing of millions of Jews and others by German Nazis during World War II

Homestead Act a U.S. law, passed in 1862, that allowed people to claim and keep land in the West if they farmed it for five years

Koran the holy book of Islam; Muslims believe it contains the word of Allah, or God, as received by Muhammad

immigration arriving in a new nation or region to live there

missionaries people who travel to a foreign place to promote their religion

Muslim having to do with the religion of Islam

pilgrimage a journey to a holy place

prejudice bias against, or dislike of, a person or group because of race, nationality, or other reasons

refugee a person who goes to another place to escape persecution, war, or natural disaster

repressive having to do with limiting a person's freedom

secular not involving religion or religious institutions

service industry businesses that provide a service instead of products. People who work in restaurants, hotels, banks, and hospitals all have jobs in the service industry.

stereotype an image, which is often inaccurate, that people have of certain groups